MW01181614

Instruments of the Bones

Instruments of the Bones

MID-LIST PRESS
Denver Minneapolis

Poems by
Stephen C. Behrendt

1991 FIRST POETRY SERIES

Copyright © 1992 Stephen C. Behrendt
All rights reserved

Library of Congress Cataloging-in-Publication Data

Behrendt, Stephen C., 1947-
 Instruments of the bones
  p. cm.
 "First book of poetry award"
 ISBN 0-922811-14-8 (pbk.: alk. paper) : $9.95.
 I. Title
PS3552.414157   1991
811'.54--dc20
                                    91-35762........
                                         CIP

Acknowledgements for previously published poems: *The Wisconsin Review*, "The Woods at Bonder's Point"; *New Mexico Humanities Review*, "Innocenti"; *Plainsongs*, "Firstborn"; *Southern Poetry Review*, "Not Dragon's Teeth, But"; *Kansas Quarterly*, "The Mammoth Tooth from the Garden," "Spring Garden," "Transients on the Campus Mall," "Autumnal Cadence," "Ice Fishing at Night," "Elegy"; *Prairie Schooner*, "In Memory of My Grandfather," "Life Sketch," "The Garden of Questionable Delights," "Farm Auction"; *The Sewanee Review*, "Bird Point," "Herb Garden," "Victoria Street Idyll"; *The Literary Review*, "Jannie"; *Willow Springs*, "Early June Woods"; *South Carolina Review*, "For the Teenagers who Stoned the Zoo Bear"; *Nebraska English Journal*, "Nebraska Autumn," "The Hall of Elephants," "Remnant," "The Bones"; *Spoon River Quarterly*, "The Cemetery at Bark River"; *The Texas Review*, "Old Dog," "The Fisherman in the Ice," "The Stone Man"; *Decade Dance*, "The Reading," "Making the River"; *Jeopardy*, "Philosophical Poetry"; *High Plains Literary Review*, "Hidden Cares"; *Amherst Review*, "Second Son"; *Phoebe*, "Storm Warning"; *Alabama Literary Review*, "Study for a Triptych"; *The Southern Review*, "Wordsworth's Daffodils," "Beggar Girl at Dupont Circle."

Manufactured in the USA

For Pat

The sublime discloses itself only in the silence of which we speak, when, by the most stupendous Efforts of Intellect, by the revivification of the Worlds, by the inhabitation thereof by all the Creatures which the laboring soul can re-articulate, we stand in a Presence which has not, nor ever shall have one sympathy with ourselves; those Worlds, those antipodal Populations, that Presence passionless, and silent dead; I say the instruments of a few bones verify a Sublimity before which no man can stand unappalled.

Thomas Hawkins, *The Book of the Great Sea-Dragons*

Contents

I

In Memory of My Grandfather 3

Nebraska Autumn...5

Firstborn 7

Second Son...8

Jannie 10

The July Robin.. 12

Herb Garden 14

Old Dog 16

Farm Auction.. 18

Life Sketch 20

The Fisherman in the Ice 22

The Cemetery at Bark River 23

II

Bird Point... 29

Innocenti 31

The Mammoth Tooth from the Garden 32

The Hall of Elephants 34

The Bones... 36

Hidden Cares 37

Seka 39

Transients on the Campus Mall 40

Beggar Girl at Dupont Circle... 42

Sudden Snow... 44

Nero 46

Hunter's Snow, Some Call It 47

Victoria Street Idyll 49

Spring Garden.. 50

Bethany Cemetery, Upper Michigan...................................... 52

III

Philosophical Poetry.. 57
Wordsworth's Daffodils 59
Crossings 60
Storm Warning.. 61
The Reading.. 62
Derridean Thicket 64
Study for a Triptych.. 66
Moving Target.. 68

IV

The Garden of Questionable Delights 73
Not Dragon's Teeth, But.. 74
Tomato Patch.. 75
Autumnal Cadence.. 77
Early June Woods.. 78
Making the River... 79
Remnant.. 81
The Woods at Bonder's Point... 82
Landscape 83
The Stones of the Old Post Office 84
Ice Fishing at Night... 85
The Stone Man.. 86
For the Teenagers who Stoned the Zoo Bear 89
The Neighbor Shot His Children.. 90
Elegy 92

I

He who hath bent him o'er the dead
Ere the first day of death is fled,
The first dark day of nothingness,
The last of danger and distress,
Before Decay's effacing fingers
Have swept the lines where beauty lingers.

--Byron, *The Giaour*

IN MEMORY OF MY GRANDFATHER

My grandfather sold monuments after he remarried,
great massy slabs to those who could afford them,
baby markers to those who could not, or old slants and hickeys
refinished during the slack days of early winter
that he paid for from his pocket
when they could spare no money for their dead.
He didn't love that work—for who could love
such dalliance with the dead?—but loved these people,
the best and only memorial to the generations gone before,
whose paths they sought to trace on the shining stones he brought.

Carrying index cards with obituaries pasted to them,
he worked in the country, preferring to the sterile city
the yellow-blooming back fields of that Northern land,
the fragrant, low-lying tamarack bogs
astraddle narrow, winding township roads:
places with names like Athelstene and Escanaba,
Bark River and Birch Creek,
Dunbar and Crivitz and Stephenson: most, now, names only,
where the dwellings of builders and dreamers had stood
in days when the forest had seemed limitless,
the rivers forever clear and teeming.

He sold them Wausau reds and St. Cloud grays,
granites fine and tight as the densest cluster
in the Milky Way, and Columbia granite
pink as the flesh of the salmon that ran the clear streams
of the Northwest coast he had lumbered once, where he had left
part of a middle finger in a larch-pole mill,

his first wife in a hillside grave swept
by the sun's last glance at the broad land from the Pacific,
marked by a wedge of Amberg granite that held each day's heat
to warm her gently through the chill and soundless night.

He sold them, too, comfort at an easy price: a reconciled smile,
a slice of Stella Brissette's fresh peach pie and her harsh strong coffee,
the morning's buttermilk Matykowski kept ready, in case he stopped by,
the first cantaloupe of summer plucked from the vine by old Finn,
whose wife he had helped move to the new Catholic cemetery at Rapid River
when the old one flooded, washing the dead downriver.

And he would return from his days with them, car filled with fresh things
and sweet, emblems of fond kindnesses returned for his own,
given easily in the slow warming days of early June.
The dahlia tubers Henry Korvath gave him
after Elisa Korvath died in her sleep at forty-two
were planted along the white picket fence behind the garden
where, feeding on the day's sun, they grew to great,
pieplate-sized blooms, waving lavender and yellow—
the colors of serenity and constancy—giving back their stored warmth,
their summer's life in the sharing of memories that attended
their annual harvest, their storing, their replanting in the spring.

When he died his family marvelled, who somehow never understood,
that this old man who spent so many hours away,
driving the quiet, sparsely settled Northern places,
had acquired so many friends whom no one knew,
who came in silently among the family of strangers,
to stand briefly, to smile when all expected weeping,
and to leave as they came, light, warm, gentle.

4

NEBRASKA AUTUMN

Mildred Wilbur was forty-seven when Walter died,
when he dropped from the tractor, heart clenched,
eyes full of surprise, of amazement,
in his purplish, gape-jawed face.
He was dead before he struck the ground,
the coroner said later, and never felt the heavy machine
when its left hind wheel crushed his spine.

She had been putting up preserves,
thick, golden pear syrup, bubbling heavily,
murmuring in the twelve-quart copper kettle
she always used to counter the acid,
to thicken the liquid without discoloring it.
The morning was sunny, cloudless,
already heavy though with promise of afternoon heat,
of the thunderstorm that would break by five,
washing Walter's blood into the dark earth.

Almost at the instant her husband's heart locked
the new farm widow dropped a jam-jar:
it shattered in the gleaming stainless steel sink
Walter had installed "for her" in the spring.
She plucked the large shards from the sink, carefully,
wiped up the fine splinters in a wet dishrag,
and threw it all into the trash.

In her blue-curtained kitchen, its pine cabinets
beginning to sweat from the tub of boiling jars,
Mildred began peeling the last basket of pears,

working quickly before they could discolor,
pausing only once, to take from the refrigerator
the leftover ham she would slice for her husband's lunch,
for Walter, lying dead in a dry field
where a tractor wandered like a lost child.

FIRSTBORN

—*"We remember our eldest relatives years later with ambivalence,
for their apparent benevolence was often tinged with real cruelty."*

Easy, she told you it would be,
like onions squeezing out,
this new life, this birth
wrung from you as you struggle,
as you clench and push, furious
in the memory of her dark wrinkled face,
her bright eyes smiling, glowing
above the worn-down brown tooth-stubs
as she repeated it, laughing;
easy, just like onions.

And so you breathe deeply, feel
the pain shooting inwards, clasping
your sides, your spine;
arching and pressing, you try to imagine
the wrinkled red stranger
you will see with relief,
hold with love as you expect,
but her face intrudes, slipping in
there between your short, stabbing breaths,
grinning, mocking while you weep
your bitter onion tears.

SECOND SON

When the second son dies, sweaty and delirious,
shaking with fever from heat and bad water,
they have to stop to bury him—the heat
too great to bear him along. And so they toil,
the three of them, beneath the white and shadeless sky:
father, eldest son, youngest—chopping
through thick prairie sod with hickory-shafted axes,
prying out great blocks of deep-matted turf
like outsize paving stones from the St. Louis streets
that lie behind them, piling them carefully.

The women, second three, sew a winding-sheet
from their precious store of linen, thick
and supple fabric of the Old Country—
fabric of generations, of feasts and celebrations—
folded with care for this journey, this passage,
in the leather-strapped trunk and brought
out now to serve this one time more,
to warm him and hold him in this strange land's bosom,
to soil and stain in the acid black earth
toward which the men dig through sod and sand,
silent, their salt sweat streaming.

They spare a board from the wagon-rail, forgetting
in their grief that the south-facing side
should best stay whole against the humid winds that rise,
that sweep up hot from the southwest,
from deep in ancient Anasazi lands
where other sons lie buried in the air.

(Second Son)

The youngest son, too young to dig long—hands bleeding
from the effort beyond his strength, his years—
bites his lip and brings blood, wincing in silence
with the resinous fire of the oil he rubs into the cut board
as he smoothes it slowly with his raw and bloody hands.

They will fashion it into a rough cross,
scored with his name, with their love, rub carbon
from the lantern chimney into the grooves, wax them
to seal his name so neither wind nor sun shall steal it,
face it eastward to catch the morning sun in early spring
before the prairie-grass engulfs it,
as now the soil engulfs the white-wrapped boy;
as now the blocks of sod—safeguard against animals—
conceal the dark earth they cover once again;
as now the distance steals it from their view
while they move away westward, silent: too little time,
too little food, the land too vast to grant them rest
nor more than these few prayers, these silent tears,
this small cross smoothed with oil and blood
that will perish in the August prairie fire
that will cleanse this land, refresh it
to bring forth new life.

JANNIE

Jannie was very small,
small as a sparrow's lone voice
in a dusky meadow, when I knew her:
small, small and fragile
and light, light
as the dandelion's ruffed seed
borne gently, easily on the August breeze,
breeze of slow days and brief nights.

Small she was, and soft,
soft as the broken yellow warbler
I found in the garden, its left wing
dragging useless behind
as the cat crept in silently
from the alley, ready,
tail-tip quivering slightly:
the trembling live thing I held
lightly, near, heart beating
next to mine, warm and dry
in my moist, cupped palm.

Soft she was, was Jannie,
like the warbler with its splint-pinned wing
growing stronger, surer on the back porch,
closed in where it could hear
its full-voiced lover calling,
searching, perhaps forgetting
as summer leaned gently into autumn,
till it was ready at last,

10

ready, strong and recovered,
ready to fly free on the fresh
morning air, next day,
next morning, when I found her,
soft and yellow,
dead on the floor of the porch.

Jannie was small, very small,
and light in her days
as the milkweed silk that pulls
free of its husky pod to trail away
on the afternoon breeze, shining
in the sun's eye, warm and rising
until the cool and damp of night,
of night that stays, of dark,
of deep and dark and silence
without voice of thrush or songbird.

THE JULY ROBIN

He stood there in the driveway when I turned in at four,
the young robin; we eyed one another, neither moving,
he too young to know or fear, I guessed,
until I got out, ushered him from the pavement
that I might pass, marking him as I rolled by.

It was exactly a hundred degrees when I started the sprinkler;
in fifteen minutes the grass had darkened, had stiffened
beneath the slanting, icy spray come in good time.
The birds arrived from all sides, gathering in the welcome cool:
a gale of sparrows splashing like small children in the puddles
that formed at the foot of the drive;
high-voiced cardinals that love to perch
up where the spray strikes them sharp and full;
jays to drink greedily from the water-troughs
formed by brimming concrete section-joints.
Came too the robin, and I saw how he limped,
lamed by some mischance and haloed by merciless flies
that lit on his one side, and on the narrow head
with its one clear, inquiring eye, one drooping, sluggish lid
even as he made his way through the curtaining shower
to rest himself, listing slightly, in the grass beneath the young lilac.

He took his comfort there, unaware it seemed
of flies or hurt, his small, speckled body cooled by the water,
eased some by the shelter, the shade, the supporting grass-leaves.

At eight he was gone, when I stopped the water.
I worried for him as the sky darkened, concerned about cats,

about drivers in the evening who care nothing for birds,
about the swarming flies and their appalling, iridescent drone.

Two days I wondered how he fared,
and thought I heard him once in the junipers:
I would not look, choosing to imagine, to hope,
to respect the small and sheltered space
that housed that soft and easeful sound,
to know this life must be his own or not, as it fell out.

This morning I found beside the porch steps
a single robin's wing resting on stiff grass
from which the dew had not yet burned,
its pale gray-brown feathers delicate against the green
here at the margin of the spreading juniper—
retem of the Bible, tree of strong medicine—
spindly new green fingers spread mutely, mantling this small sign.
Perverse comfort, to know.

HERB GARDEN

—For John Robinson

The sun warms the herbs that thrive here,
their pungent oils released by the heat
rising to mix with the heavy scent of rose
that falls, spreading, from the broad
pansy faces of blood-red blooms the size of fists,
from deep yellow heads dense as walnuts, and as small,
from the single white rose of remembrance—
rose of York that rises on its tough and woody stalk
on a rise in the northeast corner
where it takes each day, as it has for years,
the sun's last rays on petals redolent of earth and air.

Here the basil prospers, token of health and good fortune,
leaves green and shining like emerald snakes;
and sage that Nebraska winters cannot quell;
and fennel, rue and lavender
breathing forth the scents that wrap the honeybees
that probe and glean the rose and columbine
and leave, legs and bellies rich with yellow pollen.

As the sun climbs toward two o'clock
the leaves are drooping, edges curving limp with heat,
their moisture leeched out by the high, clear sun:
all but rosemary, herb of remembrance
that poor, mad Ophelia strew for her dead father:
rosemary, that spreads and flourishes among the stiff-thorned roses,
whose tough and narrow leaves hold the sharpest oils,

14

the pungency that fed and flamed in sacrificial fires
that wrapped the limbs of young-killed lambs
in lands and ages lying far, remote from here —
distant, draped in night now while this sun descends,
past its zenith, sinking, fading from this garden.

OLD DOG

What am I to do with you, then?
Half blind, nearly toothless, bony paws waggling in dream-chase,
you lie there, who cannot even walk
some days, when the arthritis swells your joints.
And on those days, on those cold gray November afternoons,
those premature, mizzling March evenings,
when I carry you nearer the fire,
your eyes, your deep hazel eyes,
speak something that is not pain; your tail moves slowly.
We grow old, my friend;
you my companion, my fore-shadow.

Is it misery to be so, to be stiff, and still to dream:
to run breathless miles now only in sleep;
to be carried, carefully, like a full cup of tea,
merely to feel the fire's warmth on your trembling flanks?
Would you be out of this, then;
would you be away, dead, gone who knows where,
but leaving my stove-side vacant, incomplete,
your pillow put into the trash, as though you had never lived,
as though our eyes had never met, before yours clouded blue,
our needs never converged these empty winter nights?
Do I love you, somehow, or you me,
or have we merely shared a time and space,
a cabin with a fire, some little food?

You have earned your warm place, your meals
softened in my kitchen, spooned when you cannot lift your head.
They are yours, and I should carry you always,

burn this house to warm you.
Do I owe you, at last, death? Is that dignity, finally?
I am your tormentor, then, withholding what I might give,
outside, with my knife, my gun.
I shall try to make you easy in your grief
for I am selfish
both for myself now, watching you sleep,
and for myself someday, some deep day, only remembering.
Sleep, old friend: I shall not be your death
though we share a thousand winters at this fire,
I gazing at your dark side, watching you breathe,
losing you at every moment,
grieving for us both, indistinguishable,
while outside the soft snow falls in silence.

FARM AUCTION

These are the survivors:
blocky women rocking on thick, rounded legs,
folding and unfolding heavy arms, blunt red fingers,
in faded, broad print dresses—the colors of spring flowers—
worn soft and thin by years that faded them,
belts that cinched them in ever-greatening girth.
Mouths set in lines straight as the western horizon,
they clump ruddy among the kitchen things—
depression glass with crisp edges worn smooth,
aluminum pots with bottoms cooked brown,
sides scratched into soft patina by knuckle and cleanser,
blue-figured curtains faded pale as morning glories
in the folds that spanned the window-frames—
glancing from time to time at their men:
their men squinting leather-faced from beneath striped caps,
white-torsoed as statuary within striped overalls,
aging limbs askew like lightning-blasted bur oaks,
with fingers missing, legs twisted in testament
to machines that consume the people, feed the land.

These wander, speaking in soft tones,
the hush of the dark-panelled funeral hall
where ill-fitting suits masked their deep tan-lines
clothing them here still as they prod the silent machines
with embarrassed delicacy and look aslant
at the white sun balancing on the ridgepole,
its shimmering waves streaming down the worn shingles.
They avoid each other's lowered eyes, lowered voices,
bending furrowed faces toward baler and combine,

toward tools and woodboxes and rings of keys.
Later, they leave in their accustomed pairs,
stained with the sweat that is not all August heat,
bearing what they do not need, what they will not use,
what each had craved in silent sympathy with the hot, dry earth,
this cracked and furrowed land lying at the heart,
because it had been Henry's,
because it had been Ardena's.

LIFE SKETCH

As Camille Monet was dying in Vetheuil,
the sheets on her deathbed wimpling her head,
her eyes lifting from time to time
from the silent, embarrassed physician
who could do no more
for her grieving husband at her side
to the faded madonna and child
in its baroque frame on the wall opposite
and then closing, perhaps comforted,
perhaps resigned to dark infinity,
a young Sudanese mother
sat cross-legged in the fading sunset
bare-breasted, her dying child,
her three-years bloom, cradled in her lap,
the feathered shaman chanting softly,
stepping gently in a tightening circle about the silent pair
as the sweltering heat subsided slowly
in the descending darkness, the sand-flies' hum
fading into a low continuo
as her sisters drew nearer, shielding her
from her husband's sight, who mourned
at the village fire where the men sang
of the great cycle, of the myths of the ancestors.

As they sang softly in the village,
weaving the dying child into their song,
into eternity for the young father's solace
in the heat that would rise with the sun,
the pain that would walk heavy with him,

Claude Monet placed the white blossom
between his wife's cool fingers
and began silently to sketch her in oils,
quick strokes to catch her yet once more,
to hold her again in the grief
of the pale hues of sky and autumn,
of earth and air as the night deepened.

THE FISHERMAN IN THE ICE

They found him beneath the ice:
clear, smooth ice, bubbles and faults
frozen in, first ice of this dry season
unclouded by snow or honeycombing sun.
The slow, hidden current of winter
must have borne him in from the break,
from the snapped-off rim of ice
that failed beneath his weight.
Rolling slowly in the frigid water,
woolen plaids wrapping him without warming
in his silent, ponderous turning,
he must have slipped into this shallow
where he lodged.

Now, face upward, cry frozen
in his gaping, blue-lipped mouth,
eyes still wide, unclosed
against the sun disclosing him,
he speaks as from a tomb of glass:
a sudden snow might hide him from their eyes
who will never forget him,
who will have to talk of him,
report him, there, staring, blind
and frozen, like a nightmare
suppressed, submerged,
suspended in cold and living water.

THE CEMETERY AT BARK RIVER

Just after noon they grew restless,
the strange mixed herd you almost never see,
herefords and holsteins together: our old-country farmers
pasture them in separate fields, recalling stories
of faulty coloring and bizarre births, six-legged calves
or two-headed, rejected even by patient mothers—
the children's schoolyard tales by day,
their nightmares in the dark.

It was just when the sky began to change,
dull white thickening into dirty yellow
the color of July grassfires, or the plain tallow candles
one doesn't use for company, that the herd
left off its placid standing, its chewing,
and raised heads, sniffing, snorting.
We worked next to them, a black iron fence
separating our cemetery and their field:
two of us, sweating in the thick and clinging heat,
worrying a gravestone into place, a gray granite die
set on a thick base, gray and massy:
double monuments always take two men
and should have three, though we never had that third
to help preserve fingers, toes, shins
from the hurts those heavy stones inflict.

A wedge-shaped little graveyard, off in the country,
its few dozen sorry crosses and markers
and its straggly grasses—foxtail and brome,
purple-crowned bull thistle deep-rooted in the sun—

trailing down to the river's edge
at the back, only thirty paces
from the crooked fence, the snuffling cows.
The monument, smoothed granite sign
of some life, some soul's worth and image,
this—largest stone in the field,
cool and glossy beneath the canopy of oak
that would shade it many summer mornings more
with tough, thick-fingered leaves,
in autumns bathe it with brown and rattling hymn.

This stone would sink eight degrees each year
on the river end, weighting its sleeper in troubled dream,
in nightmare of crushing, of suffocation;
someone would have to come every third year or so,
lift the sag-end with iron prybars and timbers,
pack earth and stones beneath to raise it level,
and leave, to return; the sinking never to end,
the earth washing out deep beneath the silent sleeper
in his sealed and shining chamber.

The storm bore down swift and vicious,
high black wall of cloud boiling,
sweeping into great anvil tops, spreading
an outward-swelling rim, curved like a scimitar.
The cows moved as one, heads lowered,
rough backs raised against the wind,
against the first pelting drops,
the powerful thick sheets that followed.
One, a black and white that stood aside from them,
called her small calf, still wandering eighty feet off—
called as the calf bawled, half hidden by the sudden dark,

the sheeting rain whipped by the first squall-blasts
loosed from the fierce black sky.

Already soaked, done just in time,
we seized bars and timbers, sod-spade
and thermoses, stamping the last sod back into place,
and made for the truck.
The bolt struck, its thunder
shaking earth, trees, field, sleeper:
struck in mid-bellow, the holstein cow
split and parted, sections falling charred and smoking,
others rough-hewn in unearthly red.
The herd bolted, racing up the hill from the pasture, up, away,
away from the horror, running, bawling in the rain.

From the closed cab, its windows steamed and streaming,
the motor throbbing with life beneath us,
we could still see the confused calf,
small head lowered, neck stretching our way,
still calling, alone now in the rain,
still eighty feet off
from the scattered, steaming remnants of its mother.

II

In the afternoon I went upon the river to look after some tarr I am sending down and some coles, and so home again; it raining hard upon the water, I put ashore and sheltered myself, while the King came by in his barge, going down towards the Downs to meet the Queen. But methought it lessened my esteem of a king, that he should not be able to command the rain.

—Samuel Pepys, *Diary*

Draco, the Athenian legislator, was crushed to death in the theatre of Aegina, by the number of caps and cloaks showered on him by the audience, as a mark of their high appreciation. A similar story is told of the mad Emperor, Elagabalus, who smothered the leading citizens of Rome with roses.

BIRD POINT

It was there when we felled the old cottonwood,
there, waist-high in a cross section
of the heavy, banded trunk: arrowhead
of black obsidian, buried deep in the heartwood,
embraced by the rings and sheaths
the years had wrapped around it.
Edges fine and flaked with care,
tangs whole and sharp,
it rested as in a lined red palm,
fragile, alien black stone signing its slow passage eastward,
traded from hand to hand, nation to nation,
from Glass Buttes toward the Otoe morning,
until a stray shot left it lodged in a young trunk.

A chance cut disclosed what had been hid:
the tree-man's saw an inch this way or that,
my splitting maul struck to either side,
this pure black point might have lain unseen.
The earth keeps her secrets,
holding near her heart the points and fractures,
stray shots and true, death and silence.
We find what we find, wondering.

The earth reclaims her own, folding
pliant limbs about the fallen fence-rows,
the homesteads left and lifeless that subside
into bindweed and fieldgrass;
wrapping her wounds as the oyster does its hurt
by smoothing the sharp and cutting edges

with round and secret luminescence,
as the frosts and sun consume the boards
that framed a home abandoned,
as the cottonwood took in this small, dark point,
embracing and encircling with soft concentric rings
its sharp obsidian angles.

INNOCENTI

—the herd of rhinoceros found buried in volcanic ash in Nebraska

Even when the ash began to fall,
the hot gray snow sifting down, hissing against the grass,
they stood there, calm each on his four great legs,
heads turned as one westward to the waning sun
glaring yellow through the thick gray clouds.
Old cows, scarred bulls, the calves bleating
thinly; like curious horned sheep, astonished at the sky
they stood, a unison of placid deep eyes;
wise they waited, the ash rising, smothering.
Without thought of flight, facing all sunward
they drank in the hot socratic death
stoic, though in ashes to the twitching ears,
knowingly.
The sun long set, the ash-fall ceased,
cold the moon climbed to see the great gray drifts
spread below, cradling in a soft, stilled womb the silent herd
where beneath her hollow eye they have slept beneath us,
their mute message held, patient,
for the careful shovels and brushes of our minds.

THE MAMMOTH TOOTH FROM THE GARDEN: NEBRASKA

It lies there on the kitchen table, stark, silent,
shedding black dirt as it dries on last night's newspaper,
banded round like some strange, compressed spring,
flat-treaded, a fossilizing bit of yellowed tire.
There on the one side, now, the jagged yellow streak
where my spade struck it deep in the earth:
I was simply planting a tree, not seeking treasure.
There, beneath my tulips these years,
beneath the flaming heads coming every spring,
passing already as the second warmth would grow each year,
it lay, silent, secret, cold
in its long refuge from past and present, from its world and mine.

I pulled it roughly from my way,
thinking rock, perhaps root, never suspecting—
how does one imagine such a thing
beneath the yard where one cultivates grass and perennials,
takes the sun, reads poetry and history?
Now, I feel its edges, rounded from the grinding,
dyed by tannin, by the hours that grew to centuries
before I interrupted, before I let time intrude
on timelessness, on dark forever.
Here, with my warm coffee, my fire to ward off the fall,
I wonder what I shall do with it:
the mantle, my desk, a dark box in the cellar.

Here, now, at this glaring spot of time, of time
that presses, that surrounds, from clocks and calendars,
lists of appointments I must keep tomorrow,

I touch it carefully, with finger and with eye,
as if the drying grains that fall from it in the warmth
were part of it, were its husk, its place,
falling away to powder in my kitchen.
How strange, this relic on my table, hiding on the printed page
the account of a killing, news from somebody's war, someone's famine:
how out of place, this part suggesting the whole.
For if a tooth slept there in the dark earth,
has risen to meet me as I invaded its place,
what else must remain, what more beneath, beside;
what great, sleeping yellow spirit?

THE HALL OF ELEPHANTS

—Morrill Hall State Museum, Lincoln, Nebraska

Here in the bone house,
as the children and other insiders call it,
you get a clear and tactile sense
of how history has crept and crawled,
on bones like hickory-sticks,
or on sinuous long bellies pressed to the earth
by endless ranks of fishbone-ribs.
You study these bony scaffoldings, imagine them fleshed,
alive, breathing, fighting in the hot summer air.

But it's the elephants I come back to:
these cream-toned frames that press
their delicate toe-bones to the floor
like undreamed-of child-fingers
concealed in the great loggy legs.
Their hollow eyes look out, facing northward
over curving tusks thrust before,
bare of the swinging trunks one could not deduce
from their pale and rounding skulls.

Here in this hall, where the air conditioner
cannot hum and sweat with life enough, or vigor,
to cool and dry them in the cruel Nebraska summer,
keep them warm and moist in winter—
here the great bones age and buckle
as they never did in their centuries' slumber
in the deep, dark womb of the plains

34

where they lay beneath their mother's pulsing heart,
safe and cool, cradled in the gentle earth,
asleep where they fell, with prairie flowers
still in their jaws, calves in their bellies.

At night, in the hushed and darkened hall,
you can hear the soft, plaintive rustle
as a network of hairline flaws overspreads them,
cracking and splitting their bones slowly,
inexorably, in the stale and silent air.
You hear them age, who lay ageless in the earth;
die, who were deathless in unvisited graves.
The fine, soft scratching of the cracks' progress—
the sound of sand-grains spilling through a glass isthmus—
becomes a faint, sad respiration in the darkness,
the black night of the hushed gallery,
as the varnished bones yellow and split,
yellow and split, returning to the dusty graves
they were torn from in the daylight.

THE BONES

These are mouse bones, fragile
as hollow matchsticks, the straw
we make Christmas-tree stars from.
Vertebrae scattered by the paper
that slid beneath my low-slung bureau.

Retrieved, the clear sheet bears these traces
of some small life that ended slowly, quietly
in the semi-darkness of this room.
How delicate the bones of mice's paws,
like bleached, broken needle-points.

It's good that I save old matchboxes.
Let them rest there: foreleg, tailbones
almost too small to rattle in the cardstock corners.
How long have I worked here, in their company,
and theirs in mine? We workmates
will keep together here, warm, peaceful,
while the wind dances white on the rooftops.

HIDDEN CARES

Letting the dogs out just before midnight,
I saw the possum leave the side yard,
not fleeing—merely passing down the fencerow
away from the dogs who neither saw nor scented.

I like having possums in the neighborhood,
like thinking of them hanging from garage rafters,
curled into woodpiles, foraging at night
to feed their plain-tailed hissing babies:
private, retiring lives seldom seen, little thought of,
save when I forget to switch on the porch light
or take a late-night parcel to the trash.
But I worry at the traffic that descends our street.

Each fall the streets are paved with squirrels:
incautious, senseless, drunk with gorging
on fruit fermenting in the hot September sun—
on berries and wild plums, soft, sweet, warm—
they rush among the passing wheels,
zig-zag beneath the cold, unyielding chassis,
fall, tumble, roll, and are crushed flat,
full tails lifting in the afterdraft.

There was another possum years ago,
when we moved here, a great, round, slow-moving beast.
We'd see it before sunrise, returning from its rounds.
Moving in straight and steady line
to its daytime roost, it died in predawn traffic—
in the silent gray half-dark, it must have been:

its body heaped up at the curb,
like the broken dogs that line country highways,
the only sign. It might have been asleep:
no blood, no split and separated carcass;
broken within, emblem of tranquility,
of the graceless, emotionless silence of death.

Now this new possum, this new worry,
lives beneath another's porch, raids another's garden,
rattles at midnight another's trash cans.
It's good to know there's wild still here,
that possums bisect these chartered blocks
on routes deep-set and ageless as the solstice moon.
But I'm back again to scanning curbstones every morning.

SEKA

She's a big dog now, our black urchin,
rescued, skinny and sick, from the wire cage
in the pound where they kept and killed her litter-mates;
put them to sleep, dying of distemper and despair
and wasting abandoned among the soiled newspapers,
the strong and foul smell that catches in the throat.
This one, of them all, we saved.

So we carried her home, shivering on your lap,
oversize bony legs hanging astride your arm,
took her in, installed her, where her coughing
kept us awake and her wailing, making up
for the noise of the five she missed—asleep
when she was not, dead as she was not, quite.

And you gave her hot water bottles to lie on,
and pumped her full of pills and potions
till she stopped withering, stopped sloughing
her insides, and began to have clear eyes.
Even the vet marvelled, who gave her up for lost,
spoke softly and stopped charging, seeing distemper
lurking dark-eyed and hollow-chested
within her trembling bony frame.

That passed; she outgrew her collar, her cage,
her shrieking in the night. Now she towers
over the other two, standing there eyeing your lunch:
oversized puppy in sleek black dress,
dreaming of mud, of five black shadows, and of your sandwich.

TRANSIENTS ON THE CAMPUS MALL

You see them in the early morning,
before the dew has burned off the young grass,
before the sun has driven them to the shaded benches
that grace the thoroughfares, the malls.
You see them in filthy jackets,
denim mostly, or heavy, quilted affairs
desperately out of place in the early-summer heat,
and dragging, baggy canvas trousers
with frayed half-moons rising over their heels,
or checked and houndstoothed polyesters
dark at seat and crotch, knees snagged out
and pocket-tops rolled and blackened.
They pick carefully at the crumpled contents
of covered refuse cans ringed with wooden slats—
gray-brown, weatherstained as their own hands and faces—
to blend unobtrusively into the civil landscape.
They work the streets, moving from can to can
like the green beetles on a rose stalk
or the red ants that unfurl the peonies,
moving methodically as the sun rises above the streets,
climbs yellow in the high June sky.
One pauses, pulls from the can a pint carton,
drains the old milk into his thick, raw throat,
and finds a discarded sandwich bun,
its meat taken by a well-fed undergraduate
with no desire for bread, no hunger for what's plain.
This he eats, slowly, with the clumsy reverence
of the often-hungry who make their morsels last,
turning them slowly on thick tongues,

pressing them through gaps among the teeth,
against gums white and blistered from cheap leaf tobacco.
He eats slowly, left hand still probing
the can's full crop for other rewards,
while another, seeing, rouses himself from the bench
where he had already begun to doze in the sun,
ambles sidelong toward the can—head lowered,
dirty fingers clutching the insides of empty pockets,
submissive and hopeful—and watches
as the first devours the bun, swallowing defiantly
and baring sharp brown teeth against the intruder.

BEGGAR GIRL AT DUPONT CIRCLE, WASHINGTON

She looks fourteen, perhaps fifteen,
posted at the mouth of the escalator
that lifts us from the subway's concrete depths—
from the stale and humid air
toward the heavy gray sky.
Her voice, pleading for small change,
winds out, wavers in the air
like a lovely crested cobra,
like the swaying, painted head
of a Renaissance serpent, sinuous,
undulating, reaching from its tree,
tempting with apples and smiles.

It is a smallish face, white and thin,
drawn down by straight light hair;
the eyes are pale and shallow,
gray as an evening sky.
The nails are plain,
short and bitten, cracked
and flecked with white
when the fingertips turn up
to clasp the coins.

They stop for her, who pass all others
without turning, put down parcels,
grub in handbags, pockets;
they clog the flow of commuters
who pause to stare, shake heads
and fumble too for quarters.

Some peel off bills, even, while old men
in dirty flannel shirts, discolored pants
and laceless shoes whose soles flap free
look on with the eyes of wolves
circling an unwary doe at sunset.

Pockets lightened, consciences
salved and troubled both by the single act,
the walkers pass these men
whose graceless plea cannot compete.
I turn and watch from a distance, hoping
she is with them, that she will share
what comes so much more easily
to one who looks and sounds like her.
When a dark, plum-colored car pulls up,
she slips in quickly, without
a backward glance or word,
as the looming men close on the lines
that rise from underground toward a darkening sky
portending cold and soaking rain.

SUDDEN SNOW

The weather has turned colder; frost
creeps in from the suburbs, under cover of dark,
finishing the gardens, blackening the late-bloomers
that started late, lagged all summer,
and pay now in their incompletion
the price of this cold-shortened season.

The homeless begin to migrate
from the parks and open spaces of September,
sleeping crook-kneed and compact at night now
in bus shelters, doorways and windless alleys,
in cardboard cartons they line with plastic
and pad with leaves and straw,
with cast-off blankets, sheets of newsprint
bearing weather forecasts, football scores,
the speeches of politicians at fund-raising dinners.

Squad cars roam the streets like mousers now,
pause where sleepers crowd each other
on benches and concrete footings.
The police no longer rout them out
but merely shake the ones who seem
inert, unmoving, day to day, to find the dead,
the drugged, the comatose.

One, stretched prostrate beneath black plastic
on the stiff brown grass of a circle park,
set back from the bronze and granite fountain,
is slowly covered over, whitened

44

by an unexpected snow that flurries for a bit,
then dissipates off to the east, leaving
a quickly-melting wash of white
to dissolve in little rivulets
that follow the folds of the plastic sheet
that hides this one, this stiff and sleeping one,
whose home is all around, and nowhere.

NERO

—Washington, 1986

I wonder sometimes, when this fragrant darkness
gathers soft, caressing; when it surrounds, love, engulfs us
silently, the pale gray pinions of some guardian spirit
encircling us with sweet waves of drowsiness
rich and heavy-laden with spice and sandalwood—
I wonder what other nights may be,
are suffered ungently like sharp discordant night-songs,
keyless melodies that grate on tautened strings
and fret the heart, disturb our finer sense.
Who are these whose night is as the day, who fly out,
bat-like, at dusk in coarse erratic swerves
along streets unfurled beneath the heatless lamps
that mar the corners, the crossing-ways
of those whose averted eyes may never meet,
never soften, but seek the shadows at mid-block?

It is another world indeed, and though we weep for it
in public show, how more luxurious these private rooms
that glow like wine before the hearth
with the polished wood's patina, picture-glass
reflecting golden tones of hearth-rug and burnished brass,
the pale and ruddy hues of supple flesh.
And if those brown and common bats who dart below
in rude uncivil passageways offend the sense,
we need not long be troubled by such as they—
mere fuel for cleansing flames, easeful ovens
fired by simple command, a song upon the strings,
a thought that scarcely need find voice,
he said, again, again, in our own time and tongue.

46

HUNTER'S SNOW, SOME CALL IT

Winter launches sneak attacks out here,
creeping in slowly from the west, spreading a pale haze
in from the horizon, until the sky grows gray
with leading fingers of thick, flat clouds
that dim the sunset, wrap the close of day
at five in darkness and in rising wind.

By midnight the sashes rattle in their frames:
the glass frosts up from the lower corners,
ice-shafts thickening, spreading up in ridges
as the clouds had taken the sky by day, like the rises
of topographic maps, cold and white.
Rosebushes, too late remembered, still unwrapped,
bend before the wind, stalks freezing, their life
driven back into the ground, retreating; by morning
they will snap like matchsticks.

A straight wind from the northwest
drives the snow in the wake of midnight:
small hard granules, first, that tick on window glass,
then flakes that swirl about the porch
and are sucked up the long driveway
to spiral and drift on the pavement
beneath a street lamp that sways its purplish light
from side to side in the streaming wind.

You fall asleep amid this rush, and miss
the drop of wind in deepest night, the calm
that brings flakes the size of quarters

that pile up fast and heavy, rounding over
the shapes of plant and machine, bending
the tops of red cedars, straightening
blue spruce boughs in the darkness.

At dawn the sky is pale and empty,
the streets uncut by tire tracks
or footprints splayed in herringbones.
Only the fine prints of sparrows vein the snow.
Atop the rounded crests of roofs, starlings
line the chimney tops, huddling in the warming vapor
that rises in the clear and soundless air,
looking down, perhaps, from time to time
at the stiff and speckled body half concealed
by the drift below the window where it struck
in the half-light just before the dawn.

VICTORIA STREET IDYLL

She caught the bus one Tuesday early,
east to the open-air market in Victoria Street
where the shops spill out upon the pavement,
their fertile wombs delivering in the still-sharp air:
cabbages, smooth bald heads in the green morning sun,
resting on ruffs of carrot greens, and fruit
like a Van Gogh canvas, alive with wild lemon,
chokecherries sour as the day is red;
and fish, fresh as gales of white peonies,
gills sharp and crisp as apples, plaice and cod
gleaming in the brilliant golden sun that glazes
the coal heaps of shining bearded mussels, the bread
stacked like cordwood on red-checkered tables,
the coffee steaming in the shops in great silver urns,
and the currant buns heavy with tiny fruit
like the eyes of fishes along a coral reef
and yellow as the streaming saffron sky.

Sated with the morning, with dazzled eyes, rich
as the market baroness—the blind old dame who brings
baskets of scallions, every day, two wicker baskets
of them, bright, freshly pulled and washed,
and each morning feasts at eight on a cabbage roll—
clasping beneath her arm the bony black umbrella
brought from habit against the chance of rain
and clutching her orange net bag stuffed with white
and brown parcels—jewels of a mere hour's mining,
like great irregular hen's eggs from Coventry—
the graying woman half-reluctant boards her bus,
to ride the red line running west from paradise
beneath a colorless midday sky.

SPRING GARDEN

I've dug in this garden twelve years—
these calluses will be the thirteenth season's—
the spade biting deeper each year,
past last year's leaves and compost into new whitish layers,
coarser, grainier sand, like buried dunes
rippling and shifting, undulating beneath the dozen years' roots.
But this time I dug too deeply,
intruding where I never belonged:
I turned up a head—a bony skull,
a calf's head, cream-shaded beneath its sandy frost,
trickling time in fine spills from empty eyes,
vacant nostrils, ear-holes,
as I lifted it, half-fearing, Hamlet-like
to this unearthly Yorick from beneath the dry vines.
A bison calf, I'm told by an expert
who measured and weighed, consulted great
black-and-white volumes because he couldn't see
it as I saw it emerging from the earth,
bearing the echo of its measureless families thundering,
drumming the sere prairies beneath my tended plants.
Bison—buffalo baby to me, imagining your
tired, disturbed slumber, this spade-point
through your white forehead, this disruption
and desecration of your grave in the still earth.

I'm still digging, still spading.
The garden must go in: I can't spare the living for the dead.
But if you bless me from the quiet corner
where I reburied you, severed though you are

from your undiscovered body—if you forgive me the intrusion, as
I forgive you yours where *you* cannot belong and,
less than child, should not even be seen,
then perhaps you will sanctify this plot, as I
shall prune it to keep the sun warm on the earth above you
as once it was beneath you,
as it shall lie, someday, atop me,
sifting me slowly, resolutely,
into other gardens as yet undreamed, unspaded.

BETHANY CEMETERY, UPPER MICHIGAN

Is it the weight of sin,
the burden of conscience pressing down
eternally, that resides in these stones—
these broad, polished faces incised
and ciphered in sharp angles, serifs
wearing from the bevelled granite?

Stone of Lazarus, sealing the tomb,
that rolls away at the single living word
of eternity, of love and comfort—
one great double monument
of St. Cloud gray, light and rich
in quartz and mica giving back the sun,
dominates the single rise in this small park
of death and darkness, where larks
and robins light the morning with their song.

What of the sins of those, one asks,
whose white-faced marble tablets jut
at crazy angles from settled graves
or lie broken and jumbled, marauders' spoil
the sexton piles in the low corner
with faded plastic geraniums, styrofoam
crosses studded with vinyl blossoms?

The lime works up in Ishpeming
gathers up each fall from weedy,
neglected cemeteries these broken slabs
to burn them white for lime

like the bones of sinners bleached
in hell and guilty conscience.

But not these.
Here an old Finn sexton manicures the grave plots;
fires at bands of strong-lived youths
who tip and break the stones in moonlight
with a shotgun filled with rock salt;
traces with blunt, hard fingertips
the fading verses that record the lives
that ended early, tough, surrounded
by the grief that wept alone and silent
amid the fragrant, sighing breath
of tamarack and pine;
kneels in the early snow of All Souls' Day
each year to name the names
the wind and rain and vandals have consumed.

The vandals who roll and break the stones
misplace the grave sites, lose the dead
whom none will find again,
nor mark nor mourn, all the Marys and Marthas
dead before, lost beneath the resilient sod.
The old Finn draws near them,
naming them into eternity.

III

We have all of us one human heart.
—Wordsworth, "The Old Cumberland Beggar"

PHILOSOPHICAL POETRY

I should write philosophical poetry:
other poets do, it seems to me, well-praised ones
who roll Big Questions about like so many kittens
batting so many yarn-balls: pale blue spheres unwinding
silently among chair legs, wooden claw-feet—
ideas that snarl and tangle the thoughts.

They draw out broad abstractions
like the tormented intestines of Saint Erasmus,
in language that moves like cargo crates
loose and shifting in a sinking steamer's belly.

Profundity is the objective, the target
at whose concentric rings, like the pulsing eyes
of parrots, we aim our arrows of mental desire.
But all those rings are zeroes piled on zeroes.

I would love to write philosophy, too,
but I should think not like that:
I would not draw it so, but hard and tactile,
fiercely bright like the sun at noon
in late October skies, like the variegated leaves
fallen and raked, heaped and fired,
dissolving in the acrid bonfires
that smell the best toward Halloween,
blazing in the frost-edged darkness
that freezes out philosophy, that fills the senses
rich and full, the lungs with autumn
and the end of things, in flame and pungency.

(Philosophical Poetry)

And so I turn always from my great plan,
from the Big Questions with names as big,
and quit the clouds of gray abstraction that cling
like soaking flannel that weighs without warming.

Leaves ablaze beneath denuded boughs,
the cries of geese falling from the darkened sky,
the almost audible scratch of hoarfrost
on the tall grasses, the coneflower leaves,
the jack-o-lanterns grinning and flickering on porch-steps:
these leave no room for philosophic poetry,
there being too much life in all these dyings,
these endings without limit, without end.

WORDSWORTH'S DAFFODILS

Wordsworth's daffodils are not the only touchstones:
we all reach out, reach back, to sights and sounds
that rise on mists of memory
like bubbles from a spring on the ocean's floor
or the shoots of peonies and bleeding hearts
that spring from bulbs buried deep
in plain, cold midwinter soil.

They dance into consciousness,
into that inward eye that figures
thoughts and sentiments, to sustain us in dry times,
in season of calm weather, little rain or wind,
to light the gloom of everyday routine.

I wonder, when I'm lonely,
if clouds of flowers crowd in thus
on others' eyes, on others' feelings;
if fields of blossoms weave and dance
for them as now for me, and if their hearts
fill up with gaiety and joy, altering all.

Or is the vision that rises
from that dark and misty depth
more like what poor Peter Bell beheld:
a bloated corpse, its feet stirred free
of the entangling roots of rushes,
broken free suddenly, rising, bursting from the deep,
whitened face and blue lips gaping to the sun
to terrify the children watching at the river's edge?

CROSSINGS

I see them in the dull half-light of dawn
when I cross the campus for my office:
bearing black plastic bags bulging
with cans to crush, with sleeping blankets
and extra shirts, a shoe or two bound

with twine or rag to secure a sole,
they zig-zag past library and state museum
on concrete paths bisecting plots of grass
that work-study students will coddle
into resilient green under noonday sun;

pass beneath the administration building
from whose blank windows no deans
or chancellors look down upon their numbers;
and slide into the margins of the city
center, where they sell the plasma

that buys late breakfasts, or cut-down drugs,
or cheap jug dreams that bloom
on sun-warmed maple benches
in parks where foot patrols arrive
by two, smack them smartly on the feet

with polished nightsticks, and send them,
bags in hand, back across the campus
to the trainyard to the west, to the rails
and unsealed cars that take them
to the next day's benches, the next day's rout.

60

STORM WARNING

The air takes on a certain edge—
the distinctive tinge of fine dry dust
sprinkled lightly before the rush of southwest wind—
as we stand here, dry still on this south-fronting porch,
faces lifted slightly in anticipation
in this fragrant surge, this breeze portending rain.
Hot: this day lies fading, sloping thick and heavy
down the western horizon, tracking the weary sun
even as a wedge of clouds swells up from the south.

We wait, pausing like the late bathing cardinals
that cool in the final fan of sprinkler-spray
before we shut it off, certain now
the soaking rains will come, will come.
The sky darkens slowly from the east,
abruptly from the southwest, rumbling.
The wind has gone: the leaves hang limp and soundless
like pennants in the humid air that wraps them, clinging.

And the wind rises again, after the pause.
The birds move off swiftly: at once
the yard is empty, the street silent
but for the sound of this straight, high wind
building above the trees—
building where our aging maples reach,
like the blighted elms that line the stretch,
for the chill relief impending from the dark:
this high and driving rain coming on,
coming in hard from the south.

THE READING

There comes at last in these affairs
that blue-black, endless hour
when the words go flat, when you think of
poor old Southey hemming and hawking,
pitching his voice in that note of woe
that set clubfoot Byron's teeth on edge,
and Peter's and Michael's, and it seems
the air is filling up with yellow smoke.

"I can't breathe, for God's sake!"
someone cries in the roiling, wordy fog
that bulges out the creaking panels of the room:
stuffed, crammed with the heavy baggage
like so many pillows, fat as hippos.

"Will it ever end?" "Will he ever stop?"
"I wonder if someone put the cat out,
or if it's still burning."
Anything to think on, to clench in the imagination
like a rose stem, while we try to ignore
this thorn piercing our stiff upper lip,
scratching like a phono needle
across the grooves of our patience.

"What if he never quits?" "They'll find us,
in the spring when they unseal the room,
dried out like figs, asphyxiated in our seats."
The voice trails on through the fading light,
through the dense and choking fog, soft,

gentle as flannel, and as gray.

Foul play is not suspected, but
authorities remain baffled
by the presence of the dried figs.

DERRIDIAN THICKET

Texts can mean anything,
but they cannot mean anything here and now, today.
—Cary Nelson

To be what a text is not to be,
here and now, today, is no question at all,
but a quietus not taken, blade or no,
an image split and paired, a path
diverging, yellow as the birch leaves
carried downstream, stems upward like masts,
turning and turning in a widening current that flows
endless, soft as moonless, starless night.

I gave her three roses; two white,
the other red as the blood of the cross
that stained alike robin's breast and anemone;
the white she placed beside her pillow.

When the thirteen blackbirds passed over,
wings creaking as they crossed the sun,
I blessed them unaware she saw them fly
beyond her window's clasping casement
where the blood-red rose dropped its petals
in the water swirling slowly, resolutely,
in the darkened room.

Cold as the legs of the compass—
one point fixed, the other circling it—
steel and flint struck fire, burning bright
beyond the flowing stream, past petals and leaves,

in the golden dome of Byzantium
where the body sways to music
in a voice but half its own.

STUDY FOR A TRIPTYCH

—Washington, September 1986

Here in my soft-lit study, carpet and upholstery light,
warm against the drafts of forced air
that scale the wall of windows, peel back
like cresting breakers over this warm chair
that cradles me like a woolen nest—
here where morning sun is sliced by sharp white blinds,
undulating ladders suspended in the breeze,
I look out across the Mall, the reflecting pool,
off toward the Capitol, round stone pate rising
like a midday moon above the oaks.
It might be Paris, it might be St. James Park,
or the Thames walkway that wavers in the sun,
that floats and shimmers in Turner's light.

Squirrels, lean and gray with frosted tails
that some Dutch master might have finished by lamplight,
hair by hair, with tiny yellow brushes:
these cull the tough green acorns
that bounce and rattle on inlaid walkways.
Lovers (for who is not a lover
in the late September sun?) pass here,
breathing in the warm southwestern breeze:
I watch and listen, imagine the sounds and smells
cut off, held out by double-paned reflecting glass.

Sirens intrude, blue line of cycling Visigoths,
motors screaming down the throat of Third Street:
the president of the Philippines,

smiling in her saffron dress, costume of renewal—
emblem to the masses who do not comprehend,
who find it merely pretty, and she but charming—
is passing in state motorcade,
coffinned in a long, sleek bulletproof
that wraps her like a tight black glove.
Behind her, a blocky war wagon
like a fat metallic armadillo
bristling with watchful dark-clad guardsmen
who scan the rooftops, whisper into black devices,
gesticulate to the grotesque train that follows
like frantic jet-black ants in chain.

The squirrels race for trees, dive into cover;
the lovers look up, wonder at the unfamiliar flag
that studs the great black cruiser, look away
disinterested: acorns fall as they have for days.
From beneath the Japanese yew below my window
rats—five great sleek brown rats—emerge
as if to gape, as if to claim their share
of this, this harrowing loud cortege,
writhe in the stunning sunlight,
and are gone.

MOVING TARGET

It's happening again, as it always does.
It's three a.m., and I'm pulling a U-Haul
through a rain that falls in white streaks
before the headlights.
This is northern Kentucky,
Cincinnati still an hour away to the north.
WHAS spills from the speakers:
music, time checks, news on the hour
to keep me awake, to keep me pointed
down the narrowing channel of pavement.

My wife sleeps, exhausted from the packing,
the loading in clinging heat,
the pounding head and overstretched muscles;
she does not know this story,
for I never tell it, though it replays endlessly.

It is twenty years, almost exactly,
and you are still there
walking toward the road in the dark.

I see you again, leading the parade
of your first litter across the shoulder.
I see you coming, moving in steady, straight line—
banded tails, blackened faces.
I feel the weight of the trailer.
Four car tires: perhaps fifty square inches of tread
hold us on course toward you
on the streaming, slickened highway.

(Moving Target)

Lines and trajectories have no emotion—
they are motion only,
the consequences of their intersections
devoid of feeling and of spiritual weight,
for they are hard and factual,
geometric, arithmatic, cold.

I feel you pass beneath the wheels,
a bump as of a pothole, too slight to wake my wife.
The trailer's tug, almost imperceptible,
says its wheel has found you too.

It happens in an instant;
there can be no braking, no swerve.
I curse the night, the rain,
you most of all for your stupid animal folly,
your straight line, nose down,
paws moving smoothly, rhythmically.

I curse as I have for twenty years
because I still cannot miss you,
because I still feel that light hit
as I pass ever deeper into the dark,
driving always in senseless reparation
to ease a soul half yours, half mine.

IV

They hand in hand with wand'ring steps and slow,
Through Eden took their solitary way.
—John Milton, *Paradise Lost*

THE GARDEN OF QUESTIONABLE DELIGHTS

Now that the garden is planted,
carrots and beets filed away in the warm earth,
onions ranked shoulder to shoulder, crests
already lifting like jays' in the April sun;
now that pepper plants are greening
in the sun that feeds the spreading tomatoes, apples
of love that should ripen as we all do, nurtured
with air and care, pinched back and filling
with warm sweetness, reddening and heavy;
now while the soil is still loose and breathing, open
like a broad pansy to drink the early rains
that suckle the hairline roots in their infancy;
now, as in all our days, comes as it must
the late killing frost, the final glaze of ice
to shrivel the leaves, check the seeds
in the dark womb where they will languish, forever
quelled—unfulfilled promises of life, of bounty—
a dark cornucopia encoffinned in the spring rains
of budding despair, the hardy onions emerging then
to mock the ruins, to thicken the saddened morning
with their rude, uncivil airs.

NOT DRAGON'S TEETH, BUT

Setting out the cabbages—
rows and rows of them in the red earth
where they will feed and swell.
I wonder why I do this,
sometimes,
as if I need bushels of cabbages—
great swollen, pregnant bellies
tight with yellow-green skin.
They please me;
their growth soothes me, in the sun
in the red field where the damp lingers
under the spreading leaves.
Down below, the roots suck the water
and the heads glow big under sun and moon.
I could put one by the azaleas,
another among the petunias, a third by the porch;
but here, here in row upon row
the great green-headed parliament will convene
to celebrate the season.

TOMATO PATCH

The season begins with anxious nights;
will the frost steal the plantings,
rusting and withering them with a crust of fine ice
under cover of dark,
or will clouds move in past midnight
and the night enfold them gently, cool and dark?

That past, the survivors dominate the new plants
set in where others froze, alone, uncovered:
these firstlings hold their edge all summer,
feeding us ripe, heavy fruit by June's end
in years when spring is warm and mild.

In May we break the second shoots
from the axils of the branches,
channel the life to the yellow flower-clusters
that hang like choirs of riven bells
split and pealing in the midday sun.
In the moist, defeating heat of August
we savor the rich red pulp
in the shade of the breeze-stroked porch.

The plants of September show the summer's wear:
yellowed and beaten, they slope to the ground,
woody branches caging the final tough-skinned fruit
of autumn orange, warm and sweet.
Soon these late, small globes
line the windowsills; the green ones
boil with onions and spices

in the great, speckled ceramic cookpot,
reside at last in quart jars
on cool and darkened cellar shelves.

The vines' work done, they lie heaped
atop the compost, joining with pepper-pods
and melon-vine leaves the slow, sustaining decay
that proceeds beneath the winter snow.

AUTUMNAL CADENCE

. . . the Grasshopper that sings & laughs & drinks:
Winter comes, he folds his slender bones without a murmur.
—William Blake, *Milton*

When the summer has gone the grasshopper
folds its wings and dies without a murmur,
who lived in sun, singing in the swaying grain
of the shimmering August plains
while the dark ants, symbols of industry,
gathered and stored, as though they knew the tale.
Yet the ants do not know
in their subterranean prodding and jostling,
in their caverns of winter and of endless night,
do not know that Life belongs to the living,
and Death, too, to the live—
that Death is Life, gathered
in the folded bones, the clasped wings, the hardening
drying shroud of the grasshopper
turning golden brown on the autumn soil.
The ants and the ant makers,
the captains of industry who train these blind legions
to labor eyeless in the black, the living grave,
know nothing of the grasshopper but to mock
the deserted, transparent shell
of him who sang,
who absorbed, like ripening wheat, light and heat
beneath a widening sky of cloudless day—
blue, the color of resurrection—
and who ceased in mid-song,
transfigured, borne into a teeming, humming world
forever undreamed-of in the creeping passages
of the ants' dark, secret crypt.

EARLY JUNE WOODS

These darkened woods, topheavy with arching maples
that catch the light, that make night of noon,
are changed from what they were,
altered and transformed, uncertain
wavering shadows of what was,
framed by an eye but half my own.

I remember this place, though: another dream,
altered itself by the cycle of greening and browning
that forms the rings in the maples' hearts.
Early flowers were here: starflowers and mayapples
fed and warmed through a hole in the canopy
where a birch had fallen, its life
peeled away, a dry skin shed of memory.

I look around at it now,
at the dark scene, lush above, barren beneath—
a scene half dream, half vision,
none of it really mine at all,
An intruder in this deep green reverie,
my heart ringed with old shadows,
I smell the dark earth moist and waiting,
inviting in this darkened noon,
while all things age and fall, sprout and rise.

MAKING THE RIVER

When we got to the river,
blackened by the downstream wind
that chopped short diagonals westward
across its streaming grain; when we got there
the sun was already dropping red and heavy
to the west: eye of God watching, half-hidden
by a fringe of torn and ragged clouds
shivered by a gale far aloft:
eye of deep and reddening day peering out
athwart the broad and sliding current.

We paused there, weary with the walking,
the miles scrolling backward in our wake
and heavy as the packs that bowed our shoulders:
tarps jelly-rolled with blankets, with down cocoons
and blow-up cushions airless and flat as the gathering dusk.
So we dropped there, on all fours:
dropped like dogs, like deer at evening
come to drink, to slake dry throats
thick with day and dust in the twilight,
from the river's silver rim.

Cool, still as the calm descending from the birches,
the ash and beech motionless in the darkening close
overflowing with the first thrush voices,
the larks' full bell notes from the fields
sloping easily into the dark edge of the far shore.
Comforted by the chill water and the pause, we rose
and bore east toward Keller's bridge,

the inn beside the East Fork,
the lush spear grass there at water's edge
beneath the heavy arms of the sugar-maple grove
where the earth sleeps warm and soft,
open to the high, clear sky,
the cool pass of the October moon,
broad dun bosom smooth and bare
to nurse and suckle, to soothe her children
into deep and dreamless sleep.

REMNANT

Crossing the dry October field,
knee-deep in sere grasses rustling softly—
empty husks rattling under a white sun—
we found the bones of some small bird:
perfect skeleton resting against a sunflower stem,
closed beak intact, whitened ribs like matchsticks
still bowed in this last parching heat
of the passing season, the fading year.
Sparrow, perhaps, finch or siskin,
silent emblem of shrinking times of bright,
lengthening hours of shadowless dark,
of the dwindling warmth of these last cloudless days
that mirror our own—clear, arid, fearful—
among the stiff, dried summer stalks
that raise their heads, tawny and brittle,
to the roofless azure sky.

THE WOODS AT BONDER'S POINT

The sky brightening after the cool rain,
Now this path, these woods, recall another time,
A young, a green time of light and warm
That passed like a shower.
Here, amid the trees still water-glazed,
The earth redolent with the dark, rich spice
Of ages, generations of trees past, here
I absorb the reminders as the mulch will drink the rain
That still clings, like my mind to the memory,
To the heavy leaves.
Every easy curl of sound weaves about me now
The voices soft and moist that speak as always
Of afternoons past, of time gone.
The walk is slow, through this calm,
This quiet aftermath of the storm:
Slow and silent and, like the dying day,
Golden in its passing.

LANDSCAPE

I am slicing a ripe orange. And as I do,
the honed steel edge passing easily
through the pungent rind, through firm flesh
that lies heavy in the hand, I observe
how the glistening, separating pulp reveals
as many shores, as many surfaces
and undulations as a wandering Wisconsin lake
that takes in miles and miles of shoreline,
twisting and doubling upon itself,
studded with deadheads, with rocks
and half-submerged timbers that loom up
to waylay the unwary boater in the deceptive twilight.

This fragrance, this sharp essence of orange
that bites and disperses,
curls about the room and seems to vanish:
like the set moon new-risen with each nightfall,
I will find it here again
when I return from outdoors, reminding
with its soft and silent presence.

My knife slices smoothly through the orange
like a sharp canoe prow through the winding water
that conceals its channelled, rocky bed,
still as the moon's rising—the moon
by whose cold and certain light I write this poem,
unfold this ragged-margined landscape of oranges
and water that slices through time and space
cleanly, releasing its scent
into the cool and soundless room.

THE STONES OF THE OLD POST OFFICE

Pinkish limestone faces
warming on the south side
bear their heat into the night:
the sun sets, the wind
shifts hard to the north:
the homeless men drift up
from the Burlington tracks,
press lean backs against this stone
facade to warm, to shelter,
to pause before the plunge
into the neon downtown channel
that runs between bare lindens
strung with frosts of tiny
white lights that shake
and glitter in the wind—
this wind that pierces checkered
flannel shirts collared up,
buttoned in vain at neck and wrist
to keep their little flesh heat,
to hold the hunger that clenches
the stomach like a fist
against curving spines rough
and yellow as limestone.

ICE FISHING AT NIGHT

I hunch against this hole, eyes straining
like an astronomer's searching the furthest depth of space,
to pull them up, striped and thrashing, from the deep black water.

My kerosene lamp, its flame the only light on this blank lake,
hovers above the hole I augured hours ago,
beaconing down into the dark, still water,
its light splitting and refracting, stars
at the edges where the new ice spreads its thin and fragile fingers.
Around me the north wind slips into evening's lower key,
broken only by the sharp slap on the ice
of the yellow-banded perch—these low-caste little pike
that heave and suffocate, their split gills red and gaping.

I should go, lantern and gear in one hand,
pail of stiff perch heavy in the other;
I should track for the car, should listen
to the squeak and crunch of snow in this subzero dark,
should heed the message of my numb and painless feet.
Perhaps my lamp will go dry, fade and sputter out,
break this senseless rite that holds us here,
draws us, like moths about its flame in August,
circling our way to this deadly, this magnetic light,
this flame that hisses softly in night's immense cold space.

THE STONE MAN

—for Robert McEwen

I never knew him, this grandfather
who stares off to the right from a single
fading photograph, stiff, formal,
prematurely balding like his son
and his son's sons: the other side
of the family—the stoneworkers.

From the ravages of Verdun
he brought his strong French blood
to his brothers' granite works:
in their swaybacked cutting shed
he sliced and shaped with them
raw granite blocks with bandsaws,
cold chisels, and the blood
that darkened slabs that gouged and tore
their flesh, that flattened fingers
and shattered sturdy white ash dollies.

He died of silicosis: stonecutter's disease
rendered him in stone. They worked the granite
dry, for want of costly water jets,
lungs and blood and tissue stiffening
with the stone-dust they absorbed,
the brothers breathing hard and deep
of the clouds that shrouded them,
that whitened beards and crusted over
where they mixed with sweat and blood.

(The Stone Man)

In the heat of Wisconsin summers
they gasped for air, heaving the slabs
through the thick and swirling haze
of powdered mica, feldspar, quartz,
from barge to saw to polisher,
fashioning monuments whose smooth
and open faces gave them back
their own, red and streaming.

In the sharp, dry air of winter
they spat blood from lungs that rent and tore
with every shallow breath.

That March evening in 1937
he was reading, when he coughed
and bright blood flowed
that could not be stanched:
in a quarter hour he had bled to death
before his wife and children
and in four days was buried
in earth his brothers softened
with fires of broken timbers from the shop.

They dug him up in 1941, exhumed him
for insurance adjustors who still balked,
disbelieving doctors' claims
that men could turn to stone.
the pried-off coffin lid disclosed him
as he was in life, unchanged,
gazing from a stony silence

as he does now, looking off
at something unseen, outside the frame
of this worn and browning image
that haunts me from the wall.

FOR THE TEENAGERS WHO STONED THE ZOO BEAR

Could you listen, then, unmoved, to his sigh of resignation
as he lay down to die, sinless, to resist no more,
beneath the dark hail of your stones?
Could you hear the deep resonant striking
of brick against broad back, great sides
that swelled and shrank in anguish, in confusion
at the twilight sky raining down missiles where apples,
where candy and the warm spring rains had showered him?
Could you watch the deep, the hopeless eyes,
helpless to comprehend, to believe
he was not to perform yet this once more,
not to beg, even as you stoned him,
as you killed him slowly for your amusement,
brutally, in the hushed green park?
Could you live so, to find in this massive life
some soulless thing, some mere trifle
for your whim, your entertainment in its extinguishing—
you who were dead long before he died,
long before he lay his battered head on the cold,
the waiting, bloody concrete, a trickle of bright blood
from his dark, quivering nostril tracing the ebb
of his great spirit among the waste of rocks and bricks,
the shattered glass and flagstones,
the fragments of the paved and ordered world
made filthy by your civil touch?
You could, of course; for you could laugh, for whom no toll
might be too great, nor stone too heavy
for laughter, for mirth, for murder
in the soft spring sunset,
among the infected elms, the willows
weeping with shame, with shame.

THE NEIGHBOR SHOT HIS CHILDREN

The neighbor shot his children,
three of them, one by one,
at home on New Year's afternoon,
with the rifle that brought down
rabbit and deer alike,
small game and large,
in the brown autumn fields
that flank the silent, eyeless Platte.

Their mother, flown to Florida
to stroke and soothe a dying mother
who will never see or know again
her daughter or her daughter's children,
does not know this,
but imagines them rowdy and boisterous,
or napping in birch-panelled rooms
with red hair pillowed lustrous and uncombed,
with long-lashed eyelids flicking softly
before swift, concealed dreams.

The neighbor drives his Ford Bronco,
gun-rack full behind his head,
up a graveled county road,
to a foreclosed farm deserted on a hilltop
and, fearing pain, lowers the loaded rifle,
gets out into the cold
to plug the hot exhaust-pipe
with a russet deerskin glove,
seats himself facing westward,

and slips into his own unfeeling sunset
as the bare horizon takes to rest
the orange and bloody winter sun.

ELEGY

Driving at night, late, beneath the electric stars
of lights that line the civil ways,
I listen to string concerti
that pass, soundless, through the air
to pour from speakers that flank me in the darkness.
But these minor-key baroque slow movements
unsettle, disturb the easy peace
with their tones of mourning, of cortege
and slow, pained ceremony of parting.
I would not be among a crowd, now,
but prefer this corridor of easeful sound:
some losses lie too near for music
and for the visions that haunt these warm adagios.

Have I lived too long, then?
I have seen flamingoes thrown dead in a bright, unmoving heap,
delicate reeds of legs shattered by fence pickets in the night;
great soft, snowy pelicans with impertinent eyes,
their bills sawed and broken under cover of dark;
bears and foxes lurching in endless black,
eyes struck blind with pointed sticks.
Do the dead know pain after death?
Does it follow them, wrap them in some other world
like Creusa's rich, embroidered robe?
Or is this all, and do we dissipate
like smoke rising in an empty Aryan sky,
like music that hangs, then goes,
when the bows cease stroking, the strings rest?

(Elegy)

I see the deer, young white-tail does
and fawns whose spots have not yet fully faded,
lying sidelong and bent against the fence,
great brown eyes open and staring
as though they tasted, too late, the poison in the bread.
Do the dead weep,
or is the dying but the final act
of that dark and terrible drama,
the breaking of the dream, the dawn?